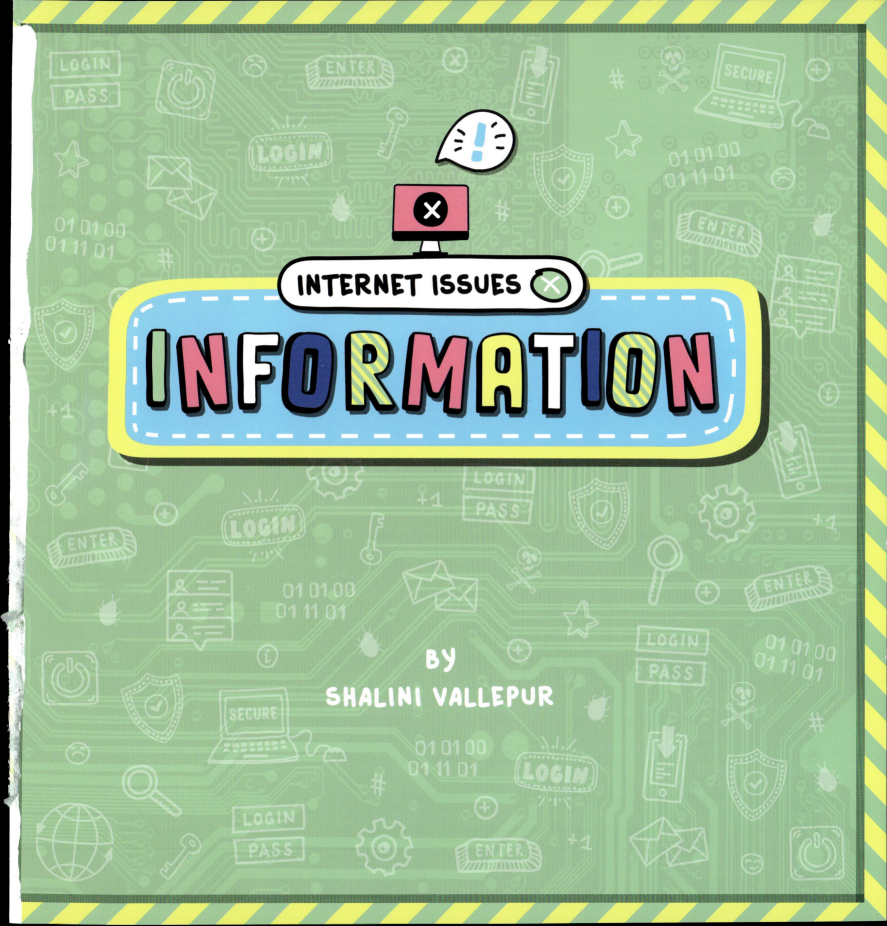

INTERNET ISSUES

INFORMATION

BY

SHALINI VALLEPUR

All rights reserved.
Printed in Poland.

A catalogue record for this book is available from the British Library.

ISBN: 978-1-80155-188-5

Written by:
Shalini Vallepur

Edited by:
Madeline Tyler

Designed by:
Danielle Rippengill

©2022
BookLife Publishing Ltd.
King's Lynn, Norfolk
PE30 4LS, UK

IMAGE CREDITS

All images are courtesy of Shutterstock.com, unless otherwise specified. With thanks to Getty Images, Thinkstock Photo and iStockphoto. Front Cover – Bloomicon, Elena11, fizkes, Happy Togethe, solarseven. Images used on every page – Bloomicon, Elena11. 2 – fizkes. 4–5 – Antonio Guillem, NadyaEugene, Prostock-studio. 6–7 – Africa Studio, ESB Professional, monticello. 8–9 – Africa Studio, ra2 studio. 10–11 – MicroOne, Oksana Klymenko, Syda Productions. 12–13 – maicasaa, Prostock-studio, McLittle Stock. 14–15 – fizkes, wavebreakmedia. 16–17 – Rodica Vasiliev, Roman Samborskyi, Sutipond Somnam. 18–19 – Andrey_Popov, Monkey Business Images, Ronnachai Palas. 20–21 – Kaspars Grinvalds, Pixel-Shot, Prostock-studio, Sonia Dhankhar, stockfour. 22–23 – Prostock-studio, Zivica Kerkez.

CONTENTS

WORDS THAT LOOK LIKE this CAN BE FOUND IN THE GLOSSARY ON PAGE 24.

THE INTERNET

Have you ever been on the internet? The internet links together computers, smartphones and tablets from all over the world. It lets computers connect with each other and share things.

+1

People all over the world use the internet every day. The internet can be used for work, to learn, to play and to talk to other people.

THE INTERNET

ONLINE VIDEOS

Information is the name we give to facts about certain things. Information can be shown in many ways on the internet.

!

Websites AND ONLINE encyclopaedias

ENCYCLOPS
FREE ENCYCLOPAEDIA

WE ALSO GET INFORMATION FROM BOOKS, NEWSPAPERS AND TV CHANNELS.

IT IS IMPORTANT TO KNOW WHEN INFORMATION IS TRUE OR NOT.

People can use the internet to share their thoughts, feelings and information about things. Many people use the internet to **research** and share information.

COME FROM?

Some information comes from scientists and other **experts** who learn and **study** things. They write down the information they learn in **articles** so others can learn too.

A POTATO SCIENTIST MAY SPEND YEARS LEARNING NEW THINGS ABOUT POTATOES.

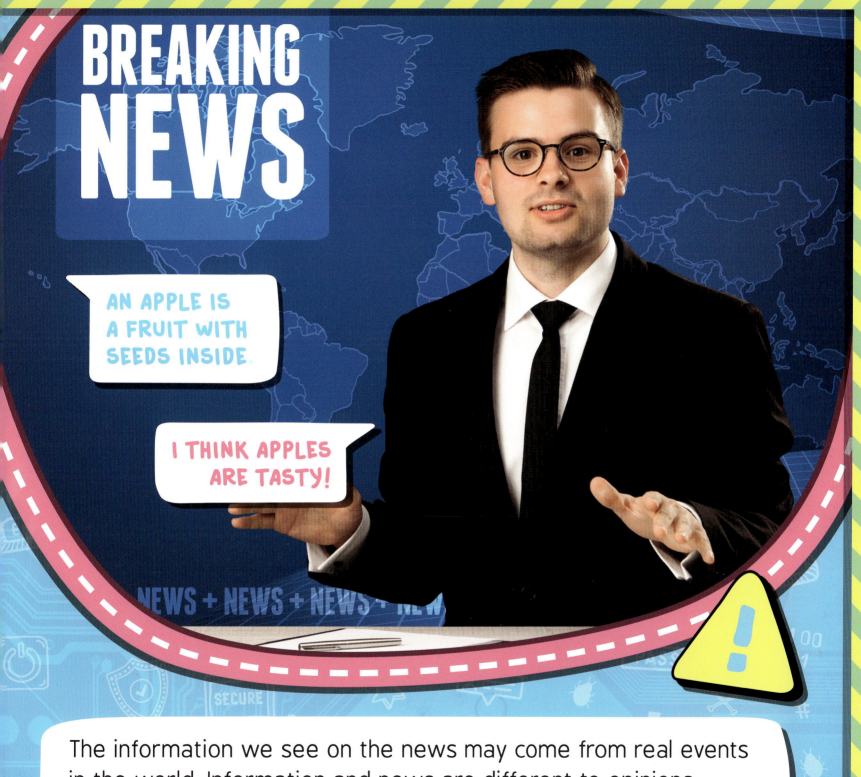

The information we see on the news may come from real events in the world. Information and news are different to opinions. An opinion is somebody's thoughts and feelings about something.

INFORMATION

Sometimes, information that is not true can spread on the internet. This can happen when people misunderstand real information or believe something that is not real or true. This can happen with a person's opinion, too.

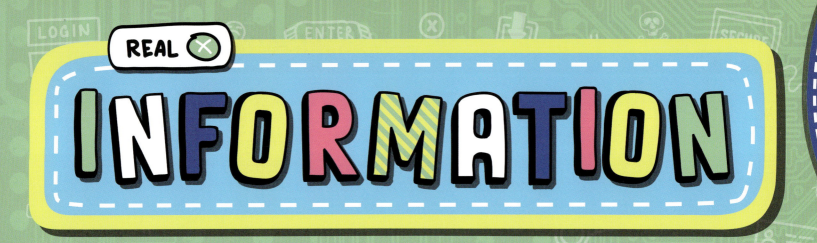

SOME PEOPLE MAY EVEN **edit** PHOTOS AND PICTURES TO MAKE THINGS SEEM REAL, WHEN THEY ARE NOT.

BANANAS TURN HAIR BLUE. FACT!

FAKE NEWS

It can be dangerous when information that is not true spreads online, especially if it hurts other people or makes people upset.

SOMETIMES, IT CAN BE DIFFICULT TO TELL WHEN SOMETHING IS TRUE OR NOT.

NEWS ⊗

HEADLINES

!?!

There are lots of news websites and news articles on the internet. Many of them have a title called a headline. Sometimes, headlines on the internet are **exaggerated**.

IF YOU SEE A HEADLINE THAT LOOKS EXAGGERATED, IT IS BEST NOT TO CLICK ON IT.

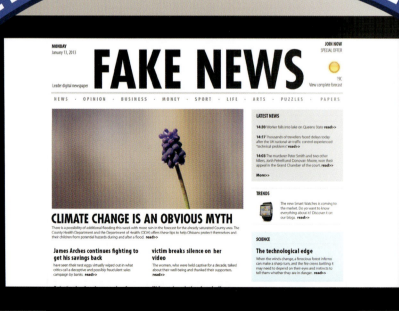

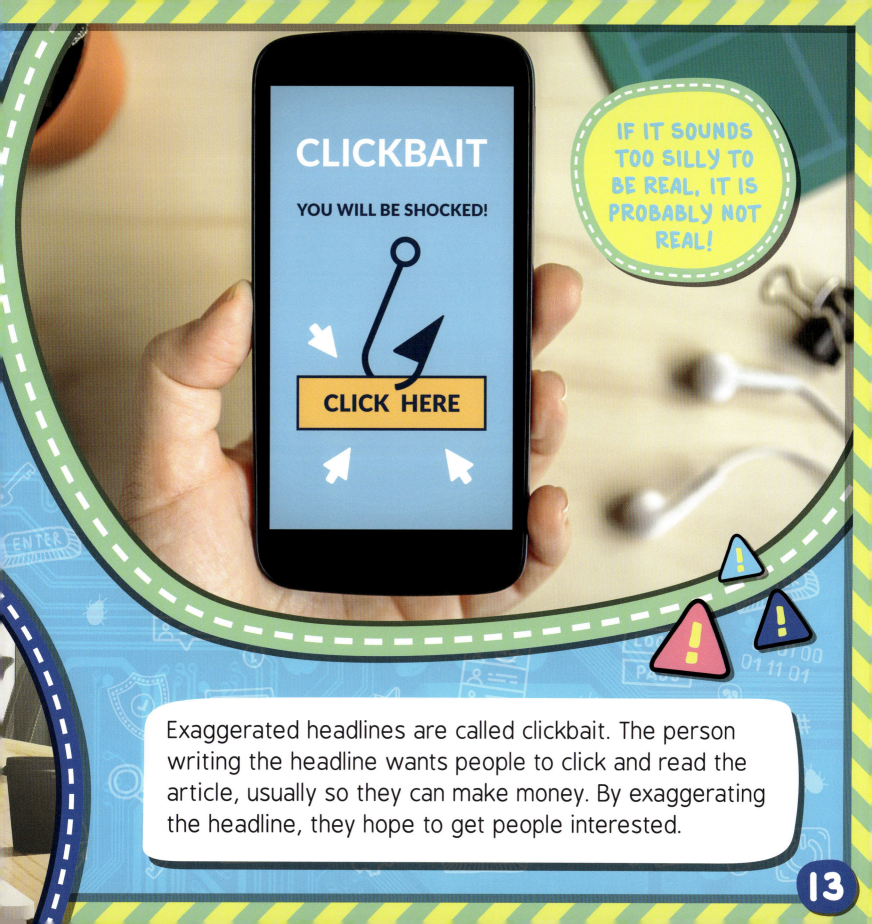

CLICKBAIT

YOU WILL BE SHOCKED!

CLICK HERE

IF IT SOUNDS TOO SILLY TO BE REAL, IT IS PROBABLY NOT REAL!

Exaggerated headlines are called clickbait. The person writing the headline wants people to click and read the article, usually so they can make money. By exaggerating the headline, they hope to get people interested.

ONLINE

Online encyclopaedias contain lots of information for people to read and research. While they are useful, some online encyclopaedias can be written by anybody.

ENCYC

FREE ENCYC

ASK A
GROWN-UP
TO SHOW YOU
AN ONLINE
ENCYCLOPAEDIA
FOR CHILDREN.

PS

AEDIA

When using an online encyclopaedia, try researching on two or three different websites too. This way, you can check if the information is correct.

VIDEOS

Some people make videos to share information. Videos can make learning fun because somebody is there to explain things to you.

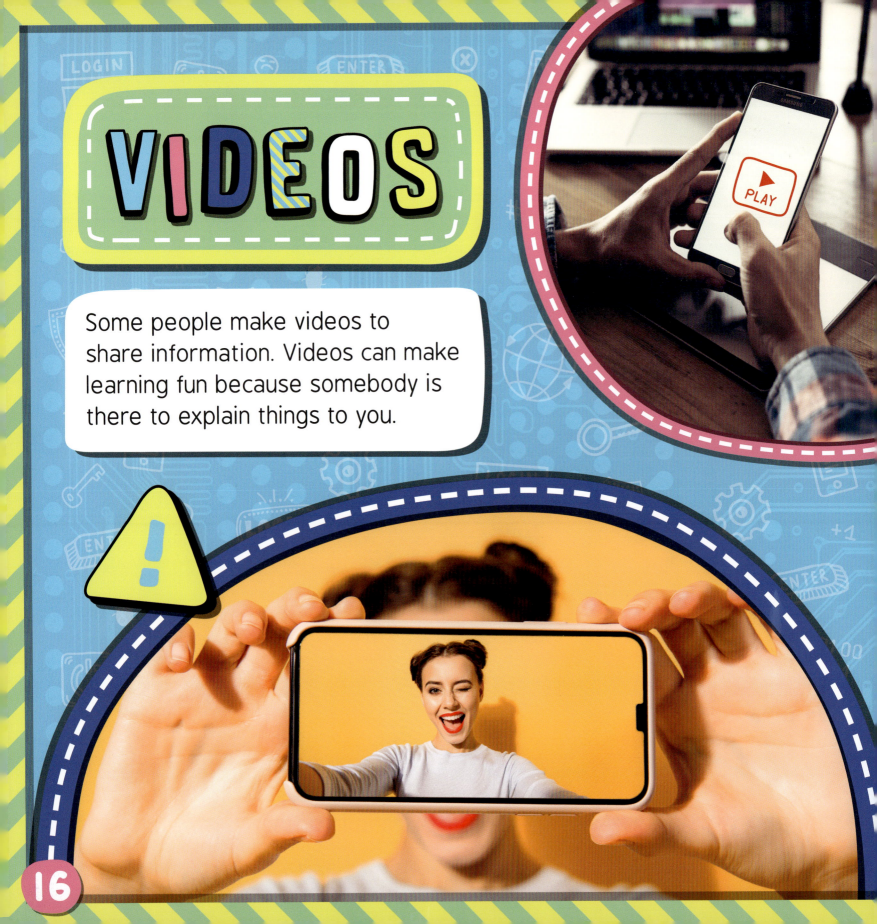

Just like with encyclopaedias, you can check information in a video by looking at different websites. If a few different websites all say similar things, then the information is likely to be true.

CATS USUALLY HAVE 12 WHISKERS!

SOCIAL MEDIA

Social media is made up of different **apps** and websites that people use to talk and share things with other people. People can talk and share information and their opinions on social media.

It is easy for information that is not true to spread quickly on social media. It is important to always check the information that is being shared. Can you find the information on a few different websites?

I BELIEVE THE SKY IS RED.

YES, THE SKY IS RED.

I SEE NOW — THE SKY IS RED.

HOAXES

A hoax is information that is not true, which is spread by someone on purpose. A hoax can spread quickly online, and lots of people can start talking about the hoax as if it is real.

GIANT FROGS **STEAL** SANDWICHES

SOME HOAXES CAN SEEM REAL.

FAKE NEWS

Some people want to spread untrue information and hoaxes to scare others. If you think you see a hoax that is frightening or upsetting, then make sure you tell a grown-up.

ALL YOU ⊗

NEED TO KNOW

Now you know some of the ways that information is shared on the internet. Let's go over what we have learnt.

INFORMATION IS DIFFERENT TO AN OPINION.

PHOTOS AND PICTURES CAN BE EDITED.

EXAGGERATED HEADLINES ARE CALLED CLICKBAIT.

ALWAYS TELL A GROWN-UP IF YOU ARE UNSURE OR UPSET ABOUT ANYTHING YOU SEE ONLINE.

ALWAYS CHECK TWO OR THREE WEBSITES WHEN RESEARCHING.

ONLINE ENCYCLOPAEDIAS CAN BE WRITTEN BY ANYBODY.

GLOSSARY

APPS	programs that work on mobile devices such as smartphones or tablets
ARTICLES	pieces of writing that usually appear in newspapers, magazines, books or on websites
EDIT	change to make something look different
ENCYCLOPAEDIAS	books or websites that have information on many different subjects
EXAGGERATED	when something has been made to look bigger, more important or more exciting than it actually is
EXPERTS	people who are very knowledgeable on a topic
RESEARCH	study something carefully and read a lot about it to know and understand it well
STUDY	carefully learn about a topic
WEBSITES	places on the internet that are usually made up of several webpages

INDEX